■ SCHOLASTIC

Stella:
Poet Extraordinaire

by Janiel Wagstaff
Illustrated by Dana Regan

For all our young writers:
May Stella's story bring more poetry into your lives!

ISBN: 978-1-338-26478-4
Copyright © 2018 by Janiel Wagstaff
Illustrations: Dana Regan © Staff Development for Educators
All rights reserved. Printed in Jiaxing, China.

1 2 3 4 5 6 7 8 9 10   68   23 22 21 20 19 18

What do you think of when you hear the word *poetry*? Do you think, *Rhyme! It's time to rhyme*? Do you think, *Ugh, I hate poetry*?

Well, I'm lucky! I'm Stella, second-grade writer. I'm lucky because my teacher, Ms. Merkley (or Ms. M, as we call her), taught us from the first day of school how fun and inspiring poetry can be. Now I write at least one, maybe two, sometimes five poems a day. You can too! Ever thought of being a P-O-E-T?

Like I said, it all started on the first day of school. "It's time to go on a Poetry Walk!" Ms. M announced, smiling. "We do this every year to jump-start our writing." She took us outside with clipboards and pencils. "Poetry is all around us. Just jot down any words that come to mind for things you see, hear, or feel. You can also sketch to get your mind going. Just focus on what you're observing, and I'll show you how to turn your thinking into a poem when we return to class."

I kept staring up at the sky, so I wrote words like *sky* and *up*.
I was kinda' nervous, wondering what this poetry stuff was
really supposed to be about.

When we came inside, Ms. M showed us her jotting. She had written a lot more than the rest of us, but she is like 40 years old! Then she reread her words slowly; she said she was savoring them, to find the ones that stuck. "I think I'll focus my poem on the bird I observed. She sang the whole time we were outside." Ms. M tried lots of bird-words on the paper. "Hmmm, the bird was blue. I want to include that detail. And it was singing. What if I say 'sweetly singing'? I like how both those words start with the same sound."

Playground Morning Reflections

Crunch, scrunch
Crunch, scrunch
Kali walking...~~in the~~ on wood chips
~~Then~~

Chitter
Chatter
~~The bird~~ that bird–blue
Tall tree - top branch
Nonstop singing
Happy bird!
Good morning students!

Place for Children
~~happy bright sun~~
Place to climb
Place to run
Place to scurry along the rocks (cliffs?)
Place to slide   rock-cliffs
Place to ~~swing~~ glide
~~place to~~ across the metal bars!
Place to roll/stroll
~~Place to~~ join friends
Playground

She crossed out words, tried and retried, until she came up with this:

Blueish bird
on a skinny top branch
sweetly singing.
Did you have two worms
for lunch?

Gilbert worried, "I'll never be able to do that!"
Ms. M said not to fret. She was sure if we played
with our words like she just showed us, we'd come up with
something poetic, too! "You know what, writers? Starting our year
with poetry is perfect because it helps us learn to observe more
closely, experiment with words freely, and discover how just a few
words on the page can be powerful. Those are important things
for writers to take to heart!"

So I tried with all my heart. Here's my poem from the first day:

Sky

I see sky

Staring up

So blue today

Wide

Sky

It wasn't the greatest thing I ever wrote, but it was my first poem! It was very special to me since I had captured something I would now remember from my first day of school. Plus, Ms. M says that if we read our poems slowly and "linger" (she says "linger"; I like that) on the words, they can sound pretty special. And, it's true. You've GOT to try it!

We have a board in our room called Poetry Place where we get to post our poems for others to read. Sometimes I choose to post mine, sometimes not. I write a lot of them just for myself. Ms. M says writing poetry is critical work because when you look at the world through the eyes of a poet, you might see and think of things in ways you wouldn't have before.

One time Tineka tipped her chair back. She started to fall, so she grabbed her desk. Well, the whole thing toppled over, and all her desk-stuff came flying out. Tineka felt horrible—interrupting class with the big crash! But Max suggested, "Let's write a poem about it!" So we did!

Desk Avalanche

Ms. M's talking
way too long!
I lean on back
in my chair.
Ahhhh! Feels good!
I lean way, way back.
Ahhhh! Feels bad!
I grab my desk
to catch myself.
CRASH!
It's a desk avalanche!
Crayons here,
pencils there,
books, papers everywhere!
I'm so embarrassed
I close my eyes.
Guess it's time to reorganize!

Tineka felt better, seeing the whole mess in a different way, and we all ended up cleaning out our desks! After that, we wrote lots of other quick, on-the-spot poems together.

Ms. M reads A LOT of poetry to us. A couple times a day we stop for a Poetry Break. We might be lining up to go to P.E., and she'll say, "Poetry Break!" We all stop and listen. Some of the poems are funny, rhyming stuff, good for a major laugh! Others are about everyday things, like eating lunch, catching a bug, playing with friends, or seeing lightning. I especially like those

'cause they're the ones I'm good at writing. Sometimes she reads one poem three or four times so we can really "sit with the words and feelings" (that's what she calls it). Then she asks us, "What do you think?" We share our thoughts for a few minutes, making a lot of connections to poems we could write. Usually when somebody shares a little bit, someone else gets an idea! Ideas ping-pong all over the place! We all get pretty excited, and Ms. M tells us to hurry and write down what we're thinking so it's not lost. Then, all of a sudden, we're a minute late for P.E!

Once, a poem about a dog made Sophia think about a time her dog chewed on the dining room table leg! Boy, her parents were mad! That made me think of how my cat, Cutie, pries open window blinds and stuffs her fat, furry body through the slats so she can see the birds outside.

I wrote my idea down and came back to it later. I thought about what Cutie looks like, what she might be thinking, and I played with the words, rereading, rearranging, until I had this . . .

Fat cat

Sittin' on the table

Squeezes into the window blinds,

Halfway in and

Halfway out.

Furry thing,

She thinks the birds sound yummy!

I'm glad I have this poem. Now, I'll always remember my silly cat and her trips through the blinds.

Another reason to write poetry is to get your feelings out. Feeling mad or sad? Write about it! You'll feel better! One day, we were supposed to go on a field trip, but there was a tornado warning. Everyone was so disappointed, but Andres was ready to explode. We went on with our math, but he got out his notebook and wrote.

What a field trip.

We didn't even have one.

I want to RIP my papers!

I want to THROW my book.

NO field trip.

I hate tornadoes!!!!!!!

When he was done, he put his head down on his desk for a while. It was a hard day, but writing made it better.

Did you know you can write poems about things you're studying? When we studied the seasons, animal habitats, and magnets, we summed up our learning by writing class poems. Ms. M says this is a great way for us to review what we've learned, decide what is most important, and create something lasting we can come back to again and again.

This one's kinda' fun to read. Try reading the examples in parentheses with GUSTO. That's what we did!

Seasons

Make us

wear different clothes (shorts vs. coats!)

feel different temperatures (102 degrees vs. 15!)

experience different weather (sunny vs. snowed in!)

do different activities (swimming vs. sledding!)

What would our world be like without seasons?

Ms. M challenged us to come up with a wise thought at the end of our poem. That can be a little hard, but we did it together! When we were done, we made a poster and displayed it outside our classroom so everyone could see what we were learning. Ms. M also said we could try a poem like that in our notebooks, if we wanted. She always says this and most of our notebooks are pretty stuffed!

After we studied Dr. Martin Luther King, Jr., she asked us to sit quietly and think about his life and what it teaches us. Then we all wrote our own poems, just words with feelings running down the page.

Treyson wrote only five words:

I feel shame

and madness.

Powerful, huh?

I wrote:

Dr. Martin Luther King, Jr.

was brave.

He thought

people should not be judged

by the color of their skin

but by what is on the inside.

Do you live his harmony-dream?

Ms. M was so moved by our poems, she bound them together into a book. One rainy day, we sat in our classroom library and reread them and remembered.

Let me just give you a warning: Poetry can really hook you. You think of something serious like Dr. Martin Luther King, Jr., or notice something ordinary, like the smell of popcorn, and words start bouncing around in your head, and you can't stop thinking about them! You have to write those words down!

Filipe, one of the boys in my class, actually got in trouble for writing poetry! Here's what happened. He was lying in bed at night, and an idea for a poem popped into his head. He got up, grabbed some paper, and crouched down by his night-light to write it down. Well, his mom came in to check on him! "What are you doing? You are supposed to be asleep!"

And he said, "I have another poem in my head, and I have to get it out!" Can you believe it? Risking your life for a poem! I'd say he's hooked. He wrote so many poems that at the end of the year Ms. M typed them and bound them in a book for him to keep.

Here's one I really like 'cause it sounds like my room looks a lot like his:

My Messy Room

My room is so messy!

My room is so messy

you can't walk in!

MESSY!

I have a baseball game,

and I can't find my mitt!

Why am I so messy?

by Filipe

What do you think of Filipe's messy room poem? Ms. M says he captured something he may have lost without writing it, and he may have learned something about himself, to boot. Plus, she says, "Poems can make someone's day brighter, maybe with a laugh or sigh. Or, they can even help people feel better about themselves because they can relate to the poem." Wow! I didn't know poetry could do all that!

wonderful

trouble

mystery

fuzzy

giggle

juicy

Well, that's how Ms. M helped us become P-O-E-T-S. She says, "Don't try for perfection; don't stop yourself; just notice and write and see where the words take you." I feel pretty confident writing poetry now . . . like a poet extraordinaire! I look more closely at things; I linger so I can pick just the right words for what I'm observing, thinking, or feeling; and when I write poems I discover thoughts I didn't know I had.

During our last Poetry Walk outside, I spent time staring at a tunnel that was next to a slide on the playground. I kept thinking, sketching, and writing words about that tunnel. When I came inside, I struggled a bit, trying words, rereading, crossing out, trying again.

But, then I wrote:

Tunnel

I've crawled through you

a gillion times.

Now I see you differently.

Inside that

tunnel,

long, red, rocket-tube,

I'm off to the moon!

One afternoon, during the last week of school, our class had a Poetry Jam. We had a microphone up front and took turns reading our poems to a huge audience of our parents and grandparents and whoever wanted to come. Sophia read about her dog chewing the table. Treyson read about Dr. Martin Luther King, Jr. We all read about seasons together. Filipe read about his messy room, and I read about that red tunnel.

And, to finish, Ms. M read a poem she wrote especially for us:

Young Weavers

To you,

writers, thinkers, and doers!

Off you go

to make great things happen

in our school and

in our world.

I'm proud of you,

young poets!

Young weavers of words.

Weave! Weave!

Welcome to Stella's world!
I'm thrilled to share Stella's adventures in writing with you.

I've been teaching elementary school for almost 30 years and have loved writing with students from day one. It's just delightful to watch them grow and discover their unique voices on paper. My first goal is always to get students to LOVE writing. But I find that engaging, concrete models of students who love to write are in short supply.

That's how Stella came to life. She's a feisty, intelligent second grader who takes on writing tasks with confidence, employs many useful strategies, and perseveres through the tough parts to get to the writing joy. She's fun. And her stories of writing are fun. Even with increased rigor and higher standards, writing should be fun and purposeful for children. Always. You'll find this to be true across all four of the Stella Writes books. Stella is a powerful mentor and will be a true inspiration for your students.

In *Stella: Poet Extraordinaire*, we discover that Stella's teacher, Ms. Merkley (or Ms. M, as her students fondly call her), emphasizes poetry right from the very first day of school. She uses one of my favorite ways to embark on the journey—the Poetry Walk (page 4). Try this with your students! Have them take paper and pencil outside and jot down what they see and hear using words and sketches. Then follow Ms. M's lead as she supports her writers in turning their notes into their very first poems (pages 6–7)! Don't worry if these first attempts are not wonderful examples; you have a whole year's worth of time to integrate poetry writing into the fabric of your classroom. And your students will love it! Don't forget to involve them in more Poetry Walks throughout the year.

I've always reserved a bulletin board in my classroom for a Poetry Place, just as you see on page 9. Students can write poems during writing workshop, during free time, at home, and so on, and display them on the board. I often invite them to share their work in the Author's Chair. Having this special place to "publish" their work lends importance to what students have written.

Stella explains how Ms. M suggests reading poetry slowly and lingering on the words to make them sound special. We call this reading with "poetry reverence." It works! Even writing that "isn't that great" sounds pretty good when read with poetry reverence. Emphasize this to students by reading a piece of poetry (your own or a published piece) quickly and nonchalantly, and then reading it again slowly and reverently, lingering on just the right words. Students will easily understand the difference this makes, and it will help them hear the importance of their voices.

I love spontaneous poetry. If something attention-grabbing happens in my classroom, students get excited: "We could write about that!" This is because I have modeled stopping what I'm doing and jotting down words and phrases about a sudden happening that deserves some thought and maybe a pinch of poetry; for example, when Tineka's desk crashes to the floor (page 10). The class writes a "shared" poem based on what happened. Shared spontaneous poetry is fun to write throughout the year. Such pieces are perfect for reading and rereading, copying for students to take home to share with their families, and adding to students' poetry folders. Students will catch onto the idea and start writing some on their own.

Note how Ms. M reads poems to her students every day, making use of transition times and "Poetry Breaks." The more poetry you read aloud, the more your students' minds will be filled with the sounds of words and phrases, with the images poetry evokes, and with the ideas poetry imbues. Borrow some of Ms. M's techniques and language from page 13 and engage students in just a bit of talk about the poems they hear. Their brains will start jumping with ideas!

Stella and her classmates learn that ordinary things can make great topics for poems (pages 12–13). Emphasize this point as you read Sophia's, Stella's, and Filipe's poems. The story of how Filipe's poem came to be (page 23) is an important lesson to share with your students: Ideas for poetry can pop into your head anytime, anywhere. Teach students to have a notebook ready or to use any nearby paper or digital device to get those ideas out!

Incidentally, the events described on pages 16 and 17 were inspired by happenings in my second-grade classroom in Alabama. A tornado warning (or, likewise, a lockdown drill or other stress-inducing event) can be a scary thing, and poetry can be useful for expressing and dealing with strong emotions. When Andres writes his poem, he gets his feelings on paper, helping him calm down. Without the presence of poetry throughout the year, this never would have happened. Give your students this gift.

Writing poetry can also help students process their learning. I often have students try to synthesize their learning by writing poems about a topic we've studied. To compose poetry, we use sentence starters, such as: *(The topic) makes us . . . (The topic) shows us . . . (The topic) tells us. . . .* Share the example on page 18, in which the class writes a poem about seasons. You'll find this format adapts well for the content you teach. Stella and her classmates had been writing poetry a long time before Ms. M asks them to synthesize their learning about Dr. Martin Luther King, Jr. through poetry (pages 20–21). Notice this is free-form poetry, which is my favorite type of poetry to teach since it's easy and has no rules!

As Stella and her class take their final Poetry Walk (pages 27–28) we come full circle and hear her final poem. Stella's growth as a poet is very apparent. Have your students compare her first and last poem. Ask: *What makes the last poem stronger? How do you think Stella got there?*

To celebrate their journey and to lend more purpose to their writing, the class hosts a Poetry Jam—one of my favorite end-of-year events, and one I'm sure your students will enjoy, as well. Students proudly read their poems to the audience, and Ms. M ends with a final poem she has written to inspire them to continue to weave magic through poetry. Believe me, employing the strategies you see depicted in this book throughout the school year will inspire a love of poetry not just in you but also in your students. They'll be motivated to write poetry beyond the classroom, and many will hold onto poetry as a form of writing they will use for a variety of purposes throughout their lifetimes.

Stella: Poet Extraordinaire is just one book in a series of four. *Stella Writes an Opinion, Stella Tells Her Story,* and *Stella and Class: Information Experts* cover opinion, narrative, and informational writing, respectively. Writers should have a balanced experience, and Stella is standing by, ready to assist students joyfully as they explore other forms of and purposes for writing!

Additional information for using the books in your instruction is available online at **www.scholastic.com/ stellawrites**. You'll find error-free copies of the texts Stella writes, her pre-writes and drafts, classroom-tested strategies to help students write across genres, and suggestions for using the books with varied grade levels.

I love teaching with picture books, just like students love listening to and learning from them. It's a dream come true to bring a character like Stella into students' writing lives through this medium. I know your students will love writing alongside her! Enjoy!

— Janiel Wagstaff